SUGAR DADDY

HUGO WILLIAMS

SUGAR DADDY

LONDON
OXFORD UNIVERSITY PRESS
NEW YORK   TORONTO
1970

Oxford University Press, Ely House, London W.1

GLASGOW NEW YORK TORONTO MELBOURNE WELLINGTON CAPE TOWN
SALISBURY IBADAN NAIROBI DAR ES SALAAM LUSAKA ADDIS ABABA
BOMBAY CALCUTTA MADRAS KARACHI LAHORE DACCA
KUALA LUMPUR SINGAPORE HONG KONG TOKYO

SBN 19 211291 0

PRINTED IN GREAT BRITAIN BY
THE BOWERING PRESS, PLYMOUTH

CONTENTS

I

II

III

ACKNOWLEDGEMENTS

ACKNOWLEDGEMENTS are due to the editors of the following periodicals in which some of these poems first appeared: *London Magazine, The Observer, Poetry Book Society Supplement, The Review, Signals, The Sunday Times,* and *The Times Literary Supplement.*

I

TERMINAL

THE station is a cut-glass bowl.
You're upside down in it,
Tiny with travelling.

Ghosts of the journey,
Glassy as deep-sea monsters,
Inhabit the world you seem to have stopped in.

You see revolving cafés, shops which
Slide like mirrors, maps in cobwebs,
Neon arrows laughing.

And the con-men come at you like squids.
They fight you with sign-talk,
Then they disappear.

Everyone is so purposeful it's maddening.
They seem to have no luggage.
Their paths cut across your mind.

Where are you? Unknown alphabets
Spatter the night sky, the blank page
Won't be patterned with your theories.

BRENDON STREET

I watch the back of the Casino: precast walls
Stained black already where
Last year a terrace stood like ours.

In the loading area: ashcans, sportscars,
Scaffolding joints, some mauvish masonry blocks,
A detective paring his nails.

A coiled hose spurts little floods
Of water on the pavement. The brass nozzle
Seems to move away backwards of its own accord.

A van arrives, reversing in a wide curve
To the lift gates where some small gilt chairs
With buttoned seats are waiting.

At seven the croupiers bristle forth with
Cigarettes, handling lighters.
These are the lords of Brendon Street. Their shoulders

Barge against the evening like a ball and chain.
They shoot white cuffs and prick
Bright patent leathers this way and that

Among the bric à brac. A concierge in trousers
Bows to them
And takes her poodle down the road.

A girl I've seen looks at my window, but I can't be sure.
I could not move to follow her if I tried.
I stare out through my tent-flaps like a squaw.

THE OPEN WINDOW

VOICES at night in summer.
I lie in bed
And hear them upside down
And think I am in France.

THE COUPLE UPSTAIRS

Shoes instead of slippers down the stairs,
She ran out with her clothes

And the front door banged and I saw her
Walking crookedly, like naked, to a car.

She was not always with him up there,
And yet they seemed inviolate, like us,
Our loves in sympathy. Her going

Thrills and frightens us. We come awake
And talk excitedly about ourselves, like guests.

THE BUILDERS

A cage flies up through scaffolding
Like a rocket through time.

Thirty-six floors,
The numbers in white on the windows.

High on the roof I see men clearly
In their yellow helmets, talking.

One of them laughs at something on the river.
A negro turns out his pockets.

Slowly a crane goes by,
Dragging a name through sky.

EARLY MORNING

I take my time to make it short elsewhere.
I finish combing my hair,

Select a cream
(In the knowledge that I'm late)

And put some on a spot
That has come up overnight, think:

That wasn't there yesterday,
So we must have moved since then.

And yet I feel the same,
You know what I mean?

The colour of the wall a ghostly green.
The town a far-off grey.

No wishes for today, except
To play it out, and not become the fool.

The mirror, the running water,
They delay the reckoning, like sex.

The basin is a porcelain pelvis
Pressed against my own.

The morning is the water
Running into it and out.

I lean upon the taps and stare.
I take my time to make it short elsewhere.

CROW

WASHING my hair and dreaming of fame,
I thought you came into my room.

Were you saying something?
I was in America, attending my new play.

The water drowned my ears with applause
And blindness shuddered in my backbone.

I came up gasping for light and you stood there:
Black, dispassionately preening yourself.

IN A TRAIN

THREE black mothers in toppling
Starched turbans like mitres laugh
As they copy each other's slow
Needles: orange, grey and pink wool
Tangling all of us in the joke of knitting.

IN A CAFÉ

SOMETIMES the owner's mother
Comes out from the back like a stranger.

She can still take money for things
But keeps it clenched in her fist and has to be helped.

She fills her cup from the canteen,
Lights a cigarette, inhales, you can see

From the way she draws back her lips
That revival withers her.

I almost see it staining her skin
Like vinegar through newsprint on the floor.

NIGHT CLUB

I watch the ragtime couple
Throw their shoulders in the air,
And you are not here.

'I am in a little saloon
Drinking lemon water
And thinking of many things
And I am sorry . . . '

But what's the good of that my love,
If we are strung out like runners,
Losing ground?

I watch the ragtime couple
Throw their arms about each other,
And you are in Germany
Speaking to journalists.

'I remember my mother,
My little daughter . . . '

And I remember you. Your body
Furled in dusty Portobello weeds,
Your tragi-comic curls.

IN EGYPT

Torquoise wings on Diamond Harbour Road.
Miss Supra Bhose on Musky Street.
At Karnak, Gouda said 'That will be colossal.'
Cracking sunflower seeds
He told us about his lost master.

ABORIGINE SKETCHES

1. *Outback*

THE black men hang their shadows
On ropes underneath the towers.

Their hats slip forward over their eyes
Like the hats of lynched men.

They have been left standing these
Few people, like the dead gum trees,

Grotesquely upright still, but slowly
Blackening into antelope, shipwreck, skeleton.

2. *Reserve*

THEY hold out to us
Discredited skilled hands they have lost faith in.
We prune them back like jungle for the public good.

This silent Reserve,
Their country in Van Dieman's Land,
Is a lopped hand on each of them.

Their hands are disappearing
Into the desert and the dreamtime.

3. *Mission*

THE Mission is embalmed in charity.
The dreams of dead
Misguided German Christians lie an inch
Under the dusty sand that will never
Be sown or broken with laughter.

All day the families of matchstick children
Shift like hour hands round eucalypts.
Hazed in flies, a bleary wolfhound
Shambles across the courtyard—ratbag
Mascot of some disgraced regiment in exile.

4. *Township*

A child sulks upon the lawn,
Exhausted by the lawn's piety.

She wants to take off her dress
And sink into the earth.

For the pink roses have twined
Braceleted arms round her neck

And roots round her body,
Sapping her strength.

5. *The State*

THEY came to us like lepers
To be cured of nightmares

And we woke them up
And showed them their sores

And hung them like flypapers
In museums called Missions

And said 'We are barely
Keeping them alive', as if

We regretted the way they sometimes
Stirred up their own dust

With a little rum
Bought for them by a tourist.

6. *The Dreamtime*

HE is only beautiful
In the manner of his country.
He was burnt by the same enemy,
Was at the same treaty.

And now he lives on a concession,
Which shifts with each season,
That he must follow it
As a jackal follows his lion,

Licking at gnawed bones
Till he himself is one,
Hollow and dry as an old tree,
Full of strange, delicate energy.

He can walk a whole month
Into the desert in the dreamtime,
Scent water on wind
And make rabbits jump into his hand.

He can hit a snake with a stone,
Birds with a boomerang.
Can play a long, sad note
And burn stories in bark,
Beautiful in the manner of his country.

II

KING AND QUEEN

THEY are taming children in the garden flat.
We sit bolt upright as the guardians
Of a tomb. We are kingly with impotence.
Our arms lie along our knees. We might
Be ravelling wool with copper hands.

WOMAN IN A NEW HOUSE

I

FIRST morning after our first night here,
Our bedroom full of dusty sunlight,
Whine of a sawmill next door, a radio
In the gardens and the noise of break
From the school in the field.

II

I am taking things out of old teachests
And packing them away in others. Am I
Mad? I can throw them where I like.
My mind is crammed with love and ambition.
The future makes me fall asleep.

III

The basket I carried the washing in
Was an old wood basket from my father's house.
I found a washing line in the garden
And all my things flapping in the wind
With whip noises. I own the place.

DAYBREAK

In the morning the birds break up our lovemaking.
They treat us like very young children.
They know it will end in tears.

So without moving
We begin to speak in steadied voices,
Careful as the daylight changes us.

When we look at one another,
We remember we have faces
And use them to be ourselves again.

SURE

Walking upstairs after breakfast
I looked round to see if you were following
And caught sight of you
Turning the corner with a tray
As I closed the bathroom door.

SUGAR DADDY

You do not look like me. I'm glad
England failed to colonize
Those black orchid eyes
With blue, the colour of sun-blindness.

Your eyes came straight to you
From your mother's Martinique
Great-grandmother. They look at me
Across this wide Atlantic

With an inborn feeling for my weaknesses.
Like loveletters, your little phoney grins
Come always just too late
To reward my passionate clowning.

I am here to be nice, clap hands, reflect
Your tolerance. I know what I'm for.
When you come home fifteen years from now
Saying you've smashed my car,

I'll feel the same. I'm blood brother,
Sugar-daddy, millionaire to you.
I want to buy you things.

I bought a garish humming top
And climbed into your pen like an ape
And pumped it till it screeched for you,
Hungry for thanks. Your lip

Trembled and you cried. You did not need
My sinister grenade, something
Pushed out of focus at you, swaying
Violently. You owned it anyway

27

And the whole world it came from.
It was then I knew
I could only take things from you from now on.

I was the White Hunter,
Bearing cheap mirrors for the Chief.
You saw the giving-look coagulate in my eyes
And panicked for the trees.

MIRRORS, WINDOWS

You've discovered mirrors are not like windows
And both are dangerous holes in the walls.

You have to go to them, arms jazzing like a flapper,
And knock your head where a window suddenly blurs
       over,

Or a mirror wilfully bars entrance on itself.
Not knowing which world one cries into, you look at
       me

And hit the barrier between us, careful
As it reaches out your hand and touches you.

You seem upset by my two appearances, one tangible,
One seen, to your one imprisoned in the screen,

As if that cancelled you. Then turning, you abandon
What you nearly discovered and stagger off, abstracted,

Freed, to an open window where you shout something
At a large dog walking past in the rain.

CHARGE

I want to charge down to that water,
Fall over with a bang and stumble
In among the boats and reeds, upsetting
The boatmen and fishermen, swim
Far out in my clothes and pretend to drown.

I am looking after my daughter on this hill.

MOTORBIKE

I

THE saddle is frozen solid.
The chronically wet rubber sponge
Inside the leopardskin cover
Crunches like shingle.

I hold my cuff
And wipe off the surface rain,
Lean over and flood the carburettor,
Jump on the start again.

A sneeze.
A little plume of steam.
The old tubes cough up a bit of phlegm
Then fade.

I have chronic catarrh, a raw ankle,
Pinkeye, blackheads and foul hair.
I have a humiliating sheepskin coat
And I lust strangely after a new alternator.

II

Going out to a film last night
We came alongside a busload of sailors
Who knocked on the glass and cheered us, laughing.
They drank to us out of beer cans
Till the lights changed
And their luminous grins disappeared in the night.

THE OPPOSITION

If I leave the door open she's
Through it in the kitchen. What heaven
As the sugar bag hits the floor

And breaks, and the eggs out of the fridge, used
Matches in their place. The scallop shells
She puts in a circle, looking pleased.

Not a moment to lose, our time-study man
Gets out a pressure saucepan and heaves it
Onto a chair where she leaves it.

Turn on a gas jet, eat a banana skin:
Not that she minds being useful,
She just can't wait to be powerful.

FILM

I am in a bathroom.
I hear a car go past downstairs.
I'm putting water on my face.

I hear the car jam still
And my mind comes half awake.

I take hold of the car
And move it back
To when I put water on my face.

And the car goes on
And the water runs away
And again the car jams still.

And when an English voice
Knocks terrified at the door,
I have time to turn off the tap,
I have time to dry my face
—the same face still, but dry—
I have all the time in the world.

FAMILY

IN the bosom of the family
A court is in session.

The jury retire.
They run screaming through the streets.

UFO ON THE DISTRICT LINE

I was on a train. I missed the station.
Chinese children were looking at my nose.

I looked at them, their faces round as soap,
And saw it hovering mothlike between us.

This was new to me. My nose is breezy,
Even musical, but was never airborn till now.

I smiled uneasily, but the oriental stare
Stopped short of me, focussing on the danger.

Eventually I got out and my nose
Flew swiftly back upon my face.

There was a slight hiss and the train
Disappeared laughing over Asia.

CATCH

Low stars, high boats,
Laying nets for the night,
Which will be hauled in tomorrow,
Running with star-green light.

The nets hang here,
Witch-brown in the sun.
They cast a thousand
Star-shaped shadows on sand.

Algarve 1968

III

COUPLE

Sɪᴄᴋ of me, you search your hair
For the frayed ends
You love to split back to the root.

Your head is bowed.
That hair I would weigh in my hands
Is falling over your eyes.

I don't know what to do
As you pass your time
Perfecting the darkness between us.

SONNY JIM

In my jacket and your jewels
The pusher is always with us.
Our little Sonny Jim.
We can't take our eyes off him.

I came home one night
And he was combing his hair like a mermaid.
I hung my coat on a peg
And it looked to me like a shroud.

Jim smiled lovingly round at me,
Long teeth in a skull. I thought:
'Some secret has dissolved his eyes.'
He bridled yellowly.

Since then we take him everywhere we go.
He is a monkey on a stick.
He only talks about one thing:
Sonny Jim is his own latest trick.

The prettiest boy in his class,
He can tell you all there is
To being a speedfreak at fifteen.
He has the track on his groin.

'They make you roll up your sleeves
And your trousers. I've seen jammed
Forearms come away like plaster
When a bandage is unwound.'

We rock him in our arms
And murmur at the world we bailed him from.
Moses in the bulrushes
Was not more loved than our Sonny Jim.

WAYS

You bring the wine
And letters from your friends in India.

You want to tell me
That you're going there soon.

INJECTION

THE disposable hypodermic slips into my biceps.
The doctor looks at me, I think victoriously.

My blood retreats. His smile is threaded to
My gooseflesh, like a hunk of bait.

His pincer thumb converges on two hooked fingers.
Tetanus toxoid flares my fingertips.

The arm is stuffed. It works on a pulley now,
Dangling there like a toy acrobat.

GIRL

From the crowded platform
Of this end-of-line resort
You wave goodbye to me.

There are tears in your eyes
As you scan the new arrivals
For your next lover.

THE SAILING WIND

ALL day we fooled around the port,
Spending the money like reprieved lifers,
We are as happy as lovers, talking

As if your going ended here
In this blue Ocean Dining Room the last day
Of a month gone on ahead of us.

For a month we have been dying sulkily,
Our bodies futurized, abandoned,
Become symbols of treachery.

Today we are back. The sailing wind
Blows over us.
We tear apart and feel such ecstasy.

45

RETURNING TO SOUTHAMPTON

THERE's no one in the bar, so the barman
Looks at me and I remember him.

Was it really today
We crowded these sealed windows

Looking for the *Pasteur* in the pink-
Shot waters off Spithead?

The Isle of Wight
Was like a tropic island in America.

Where is it Dad?
There it is. Boat. Water. Fire.

Our table was 'Reserved for Agents'
So you put the sign in your pocket.

Have you got a biscuit sir? Look,
The *QE2* disappearing behind that pier.

I can't see it. Nor can I.
Someone said: look at the ugly ship, darling.

But the *Pasteur* was freshly-painted white
And we were happy as children, staring

Proudly along its solving shape
As the hull drove its name between us.

GONE AWAY

WE leave each other and the habits
Fall away like sight of land.

Now I am featureless
And you are infinite again.

SUSSEX

BROKEN mauve lightning.
The rooks
Explode upwards
Out of the mauve bracken.

THE ELEPHANT IS OVERTURNED

I

THE elephant is overturned
And the snowstorm smashed.

The farm is scattered
And the mini-bricks

Lie old and dazzling
As jewels on the linoleum.

I let things lie.
It seems like donkey's years

Since my family went home.
From where they are

I think they look at me with love
And wonder why my future doesn't take.

II

Some hand
Has cut a section through my house.

Our bedroom is an open dig where we are petrified,
Naked as the lovers of Pompei,

Sunk in history, three thousand years
Beyond the day we walked in there,

Perhaps passionately, perhaps
For fun. Now we shall never know.

LAST PERFORMANCE

I help you take off your coat
And feel the gesture lock in me.

You look contented with your false lover.
You are genial as a stray dog.

IN THE VACUUM

I

His Carnaby Street frock coat
Reminds him of himself.

Flared trousers hold up
The dead courtier.

It's hard to imagine
Him choosing a coat today.

His ghost has sucked him
Into its vacuum.

He's naked in there,
Getting smaller.

II

They're going to garotte him again.
He's buzzing with horror.

The human honeycomb
Is trying to replace itself.

The hive is empty.
Bees fly out of his ears.

DRIVING IN FRANCE

Road soft as hair,
My shoulder brushes the avenue.

My head might nod to sleep
In the leaves which batter like windsails.

My eyes might reap the long fields.
I would be buried in the clouds.

WITHDRAWAL

THE spare-part man is breaking up.
Only his clothes
Hide the year-old accident
Looming like a becalmed hulk in his eyes.

Reconstituted from memory,
He is not an accurate model of himself.
His weathered skull
Can barely hold onto his hair.

The little faults
Are wearing holes in his silk skin.
He has had to close down whole areas of pain,
Like disused wings of a childhood.

If he moves at all, the atoms
Fizz and scream at him and some
Burst spluttering over the top. His life
Is something from a schoolboy's science kit.

The antidote is too far back for him to know.
He's fossilized,
Crumbling chalkily in space.
The little bits of him are wild geese.

IN PATIENT

I can find no argument, or even
Dumb insolence to comfort me
In this empty house like an aquarium.
Everything is seen to. They bring me tea

At all the right times, people
From under the stairs with rosy cheeks
And curls, whose steps are so gentle
You never hear them unless a board creaks

Or a door slams. I don't know why,
But after lunch they put a deckchair under a lime
And want me to sit there breathing quietly
Until I hear a bell go in the compound . . .

FEBRUARY THE 20th STREET

A coincidence must be
Part of a whole chain
Whose links are unknown to me.

I feel them round me
Everywhere I go: in queues,
In trains, under bridges,

People, or coincidences, flukes
Of logic which fail
Because of me, because

We move singly through streets,
The last of some sad species,
Pacing the floors of zoos,

Our luck homing forever
Backward through grasses
To the brink of another time.